The Strategic Mind
Of
A Young Legend

The Strategic Mind
Of
A Young Legend

A College Graduate at 16 Changes the World

One Word at a Time

AMARA LEGGETT

Connect with the Author

AYoungLegend.com
Contact@AyoungLegend.com
Facebook: @TheAYoungLegend
Instagram: @A.Young.Legend
YouTube: A Young Legend

Dedication

To my Great-Grandfather

Aljunius Leggett

Although I never had the honor to meet you,

you live on in my dreams

Table of Contents

Chapter 1

It's Only the Beginning

"You have no idea what you are capable of until you try."

- Unknown

I stepped outside of the steel elevator and began walking down the bright, white hallways with the hope that today would be a great day. I looked to my left and noticed a reflective piece of glass in the door that opened to a lab classroom. Staring a few seconds more, I began to see a baby cougar appear with determination in its eyes and ready to make a difference in the world. Each square I passed on the white tile floors, my mother was beside me. When we finally reached the numbered classroom that I was expected to remain in for two long and unusual hours, my mother ushered me inside. As soon as I touched the chilling door handle, I cried. My heart felt as though it were pounding out of my chest and I realized that I just needed to breathe. Suddenly, a negative thought found its way into my head shouting "you cannot do this." I knew that I had to because any moment later I would be late to my first class.

I pushed on the heavy door and walked inside the classroom of my next college class at fourteen years old. Strangely, this class felt different from the college class I was taking at my high school. There was a chance that the weighted textbooks in my bag would relieve some of the pressure of assuming this class felt different. I discovered a seat along the wall that was paired with a computer and my professor began her lecture. I found myself sitting next to two ladies much older than I. I felt like a mouse lost in the jungle, darting the large raindrops and birds perched on the tall branches. The professor said that we would begin with an exercise to introduce ourselves to each other. I chose to partner with the lady sitting to my right, who seemed to smile at me more than ordinary. We dove into discussing our plan of study and where we were from. Next, the question I now dreaded, "Tell me something interesting about yourself" said my new class partner.

I must have had adrenaline running through my veins, confusing my body's nervousness for excitement because I blurted out that I was fourteen years old. I do not remember much that happened following but when it came time to present our partner's findings to the class all I heard were gasps. "I wish I'd started taking college classes that early because then I would not be in debt up to my knees," another student stated across the room.

I did not anticipate telling my age would lead to such a challenging semester of constantly having to prove my worth and maturity. Most of my semester was spent helping others improve their writing skills. One student shared how she graduated from a school district that never focused on academic writing and did not take the time to personally develop the students' writing efforts. Once, I was assisting another on reviewing her essay before the submission deadline, the professor motions for my attention and states "as a high schooler you may not understand when to stop talking, but I would like everyone to work on their own." That was the first indication that my age would determine my success in this class. Several other instances like this occurred, like again being mentioned by my age when the professor is explaining a story about confidence and embarrassment for males versus females because "you could not possibly comprehend a story like that yet," she said to me

Sadly, my enjoyment for experiencing college as a teenager was leaving me, until the students said things to me that would change my life forever. I realized that I was walking into class with a feeling of wanting this semester to be over when suddenly the student I previously helped sat across from me and thanked me for always helping them with their assignments. Another student proceeded to tell me that I have a great amount of courage and strength to do what I did at fourteen years old. Also, congratulating me for working hard on my education as they felt they should have at my age. I looked around the room to find all my classmates began nodding their heads in agreement to signal that I am on the right path to success. Once the discussion fizzled out and the teacher entered the room, I realized that this would be the only time that I decided to bring up my age in class. Age is just a number when someone does not live by and work based on the limits placed by society.

After this first on-campus college class, I made a promise to myself to never mention my age to a professor unless very necessary. Being referenced many times by my age clearly had no merit to entering high school with seven completed credits and taking advantage of a program for students to begin college classes early. Two years later I graduated with an Associate of Science Degree and with my High School Diploma at sixteen years old. Since then, my age has only been used to inspire people. The potential that kids must be great extends far beyond society, rules, expectations, and stereotypes. If students are given the right mentorship and resources to find their passion and soar, you will be surprised at what they do with it.

I spent six semesters walking on the same college campus and began recognizing friends that I knew in middle and elementary school. Many of them were once bullied for their appearances, intelligence, and limited access to the latest technologies. The dual enrollment students walked the halls of my local community college with bright smiles on your faces and large books in their bags. Their confidence beamed and for once I saw what I always expected to see in school. I even saw a kid that I went to middle school with, who was working at the college bookstore. I walked up to the counter to check out my textbooks for the last semester of my program before I graduated and noticed a familiar face. She recognized me as well and we began to catch up. She was playing a sport, working an internship, and all her classes were at the college. When she handed me my receipt, I made sure to leave her with my business card. I told her that I would love to feature her on my blog because she owned an amazing story that people should know. She was the first person that I knew taking advantage of college sports even though she was sixteen years old.

It became obvious to me that my age can truly inspire people by sharing my story with others of how I started on my business journey. Walking into a Staples stores, I brought in my bright red laptop that seemed to carry my entire life. I smiled with a grin from one ear to the other and approached the print service counter anxious to request a large order. Once again, my mother stood beside me to explain the technical details of my request to the store clerk. We sat down in the office chair section of the store to patiently wait for fresh, fancy paper to shoot out of the printer with a count of 250. I swiveled around in the mesh back chair wishing the ground below would remain still until I heard the magic words. "Your order is ready" my mother stated with excitement in her voice. We spent almost every day for a month sitting at the tables outside of Starbucks perfecting the placement, fonts, and content of my business cards. I attempted to balance myself while walking to the left corner of the store, I prayed that the alignment of my logo would be just right. The young man who made sure to preview my design before sending it into the expensive machine, slid the crisp red and white box over to me. I opened one corner and then the other to eventually see my brand on glossy three and one half by two-inch sheets of cardstock.

The future businesswoman that I am, felt the urge to try my first elevator pitch at this very moment. "Are you or someone you know still enrolled in high school? I have a blog AYoungLegend.com where I document my experiences as I will soon graduate high school and college at sixteen years old. Here is my business card. Make sure to check it out and subscribe!" I did not say it as perfectly as you read it here. There were several hiccups and stutters, but I believe I got the message across. He read the back of my card and looked me in the eyes to say "Actually I do! My sister is still in high school and she needs to hear your story. I wish I could do this because I am working so hard here to pay for my college education and trying to juggle them both. I will make sure to share this on Snapchat." After my first business conversation, I felt satisfaction in being able to help his sister just by writing my story on a few blog posts. The moment that I finally sat in the passenger seat of the car after thirty minutes of patiently waiting in the store, I knew this was only the beginning of A Young Legend.

My first pitch was the start of my rhythm as a blogger trying to build my brand. Every time I shake someone's hand or submit my resume, I now give a fluid, strong, and persuasive sales speech. I would not have known the feeling of telling my story to strangers and handing them what I considered an expensive and well-designed business card until I tried it the first time. I would have been frightened to think a child would not benefit from seeing another child do what they have always wanted to if it were not for that student working hard at the store to pay for his college education. Occasions like that are the unscripted moments that can show if you are on the right path. I have since had kids and parents reach out to me through my blog because of my brand to seek advice for beginning and being successful with dual enrollment. Every voice heard is my moment to appreciate the work I have done to build a brand around a great cause.

The first time that I was able to extend my brand and share my story was with my school. My high school was hosting its annual "Peace Talk" for students and teachers to share personal stories and provide inspirational value on a topic of their choice. I emailed the staff member managing the speaker proposals and shared my experiences about College Credit Plus' potential to provide an opportunity for students to take college classes for free as young as in seventh grade. I requested permission to send a mass email to the school regarding my topic of discussion. Also, I made an AYoungLegend.com t-shirt and wore it with a blazer, pairing that with a bowl of candy and a stack of flyers. I spoke my heart out about the program and the doors it has opened for me in two separate 30-minute sessions. I answered questions and asked for feedback. In total, I inspired about five students and six teachers. I predicted more success, but the responses I received were worth more than the number of subscribers I saw in my email that day. I then knew why high school students were not fully pursuing the program as I had. They thought their intelligence was pale in comparison to "overachievers like me." I then realized that the direction of my brand needed to shift to inspiring kids to accomplish what may seem impossible because they all had the potential to be Young Legends of their school and communities.

It was difficult to discover how I can make an impact on the world, but I found my purpose by being aware of how my story was unique. If you are looking for some direction as to what areas to begin, attempting different things is a time of self-reflection, self-awareness, and self-discovery. Before you make an excuse of "I do not know how to learn if I do not have a teacher to teach me," you have something that you underestimate. Your phone, tablet, and laptop are great methods of getting access to knowledge, if you do not have the opportunity to a take a class. I was able to learn seven programming languages HTML, CSS, JavaScript, jQuery, PHP, SQL, and Python through Codecademy, which is a website that offers free courses to learn a language and use them in real-world applications. The internet provides more opportunities for you to be a great professor and student because you are disciplined enough to teach yourself and commit to a goal.

I had not learned the skill of blogging when I started my business, but I knew that I would, and that prediction was enough support for me to just go for it. I created a free website and purchased a $0.99 domain. I ensured that ten blog posts were written before I published my website.

To begin creating your business today, begin with the simple tasks and take it one step at a time. If you would like to be a photographer, you can take photos with your phone and start building a portfolio on Instagram. It is just as easy to create a photo portfolio as it is to be a published author. Open a document on your laptop and begin outlining how many chapters needed and the number of stories told to provide value to your readers. The book can be self-published or with a publishing company to sell your writings. Every idea that I have mentioned can be successful if you simply start your journey. Do not wait until you can be better prepared. Do at least one task today to help you soon achieve your goal. Create a social media business account to begin showcasing how you are making a difference in your community and school. Next, observe the marketing and promotion ideas of successful influencers to build your brand that changes the world.

I had no idea how to build a brand and grow my blog audience, but I knew that the business would evolve as I would over time. If you have an amazing story to share, a website is a great platform to blog, vlog, sing, dance, or speak for people around the world to see. If you desire to be a professional speaker, audition to speak at your local TEDx event or present at your school. I have now been blogging for more than one year, but I recently spoke at a TEDx event and fell in love with standing on the red carpet speaking my heart out to an audience. Although I discovered a passion for blogging, I also found enjoyment in speaking as an addition to my brand. Leave room in your thoughts to continue trying new experiences even after you discover your initial interest.

Sometimes a cause that you may see on television lights a fire inside of you to create an organization to support a community in need. Do not wait on college to teach you how to be an attorney and to begin representing your city. Teaching coding, managing financial investments, and learning how to leverage social media platforms for businesses are all things you can teach yourself.

Lessons learned in college can also be uncovered when you start doing what you love to do.

Chapter 2

Manifest Your Worth

"Set a goal so big that you cannot achieve it until you grow into the person who can."

- Anonymous

I stood on the side of the stage watching people fly past me leaving me tremendously nervous as I watched their shadows fade. Speaker coaches, directors, and performers were dressed up in fitted blazers, brown leather shoes, and beautiful Irish costumes. I watched the previous speaker as she spoke and I almost teared up because this was all really happening. While the next microphone was being hooked to the back of my white skirt and tucked underneath my blazer, I remembered how hard I worked to get to this spot. Before I graduated from high school and college in December of 2017, I made a goals list for 2018. Number one was graduation and number two was to do a Ted Talk. I never imagined that I would complete it in 2018 and at seventeen years old, but here

I stand. I heard my name mentioned and I realized show time was here and now.

The sound of people applauding, and my heart beat drowned the anxiousness I possessed. I thought back to when the speaker before me went to the stage, she told me that I should imagine myself after my talk. I closed my eyes to see myself walking off the stage with a smile and the pure satisfaction that I was there to provide value which helped me achieve the impossible. I began walking to the stage stopping promptly on the red, circle carpet. I turned to my audience, clicked the button on the remote displaying my first image, and commenced telling my story to the world.

I said my last words "It just goes to show if I can do it, you can definitely do it. Thank you!". I felt emotional because during the nine minutes that I was on the red circle, I had time for contemplation. At that moment, I believed I was on top of the world and in control of my own life. I waited so long to share my story amongst a larger platform besides family. I needed to tell my story of determination and hard work that allowed me to achieve something so amazing. I sensed that the universe was speaking to me, telling me to continue speaking and inspire people to accomplish their own version of success. I had not known that writing down my goal on a simple piece of paper would begin to form opportunities to achieve what was set out, such as an audition at TEDx New Albany. An email blast went out of all the students in my high school about the open mic auditions. I knew I had to attend. I found myself on stage wearing a sweatshirt that I purchased from my college choice on a college tour the previous summer. I explained my story without structure, a plan, or end in sight. When I finished, I heard amazement from the audience. The youth team pounded me with questions of how I did it. I realized at that moment, I would have to outline how I made it happen and make it simpler for others to apply in their life. Of course, all of this, if I were accepted to speak in the event.

I can recall the earliest occurrence I knew that planning can help me achieve my most challenging goals while in high school. Once I completed my first semester of college classes, I outlined a plan to see how early I could graduate and discovered that it could be at sixteen years old if I worked hard and stuck to my plan. Each completed semester, I came back to this written plan to see what more I needed to complete to stay on track. I ran into roadblocks that forced me to go back to the drawing board. I walked into my college counselor's office to schedule classes, only to hear her say "You are not on track to graduate" simply because of one class. I spent two years specifically planning the correct classes to avoid any dilemmas. The counselor shared that I had taken a programming class that did not apply to my Associate of Science degree. My heart dropped with frustration and sadness because I was determined to graduate on time. I previously applied to further my education at new colleges for the semester directly after graduation. I was truly ready to move on and begin taking classes that applied to my computer science major. Despite the situation, options were discussed to spend another semester to spread out the twenty-one credits I needed to graduate. After almost two weeks of debating, one class was excused. I then only needed to take eighteen credits, yet that was more than I had ever taken at one time. Long story short, I eventually enrolled in five classes and juggled that with an internship, blogging, as well as preparing to move. It was an overwhelming semester, but I do not regret the decisions I made to make sure my plan was accomplished. My graduation has opened many opportunities to help me build a successful brand.

After the accomplishment of my last two plans, I decided to create a new one for 2018. This time I divided it into months and included other business ventures that I want to be executed to continue building my brand. Each month I planned a specific number of events and organizations I want to speak to along with the number of pages I wanted complete for this book. I feel like I am flying blind when I do not have a plan. Sometimes that could lead to the failure of your goal. For my college schedule, it was helpful to have it split into semesters. But monetary and action goals can be broken into months. I work best with semi-annual or year-long goals because I cannot anticipate exactly how my life will be in three years.

Begin to outline how much money you want to make for that month or people you want to impact, then break it down further into how many products you need to sell to fulfill that number. You can also think about it as if you have a C in your math class and you want to reach an A by the end of the school year. Write out the tasks you will complete to raise it by a letter grade every two months and how you plan to achieve it. An example would be, attending tutoring each quiz week for two hours and then have a study group to meet thirty minutes every other week.

Goals books are very helpful when outlining because it gives you plenty of room to think and write out every detail. The first page could be the overall number or grade you hope to achieve. Then each page goes in depth about the methods needed to try and donate the first 1,000 books for your organization or people you need to pitch to speak at an event for the following month. This journal can also be taken with you everywhere so that you can reference it before you make a big decision to be featured in an online magazine and hold yourself accountable. The journal also allows for improvements to be made when plans change, and you must step back to re-evaluate your end goal. A goals book is your exercise of manifestation, which means that when you believe it will be done and opportunities will come for you to carry it out. Keep in mind that if you find yourself lost in the goal and do not see yourself meeting the smaller goals, find a way to make your own opportunities.

"What you feel, you attract. What you imagine, you create."
- Buddha

My goals books are the source of my inspiration. It is a plan sheet that needed to be filled. My first goal was to write out a plan for a game I was programming and it was the foundation for the elements I wanted to include and get it published on the phone application store. I envisioned a strategy to begin building my A

Young Legend brand with shirts and impactful newsletters for people when they subscribed to my blog. I eventually jumped to my college search and the several tasks I had to complete to get scholarships and enroll in my top choice. After the college selection process was complete, I went back to using the book for my brand building. I began to see the potential for my business to form around Young Legends like you.

One relaxing method I suggest is to also manifest what you desire. Do not just write down your goal but imagine how you will feel after you accomplish your set plan. One night, I finished sending emails, pitching events, and engaging on social media, when I laid down to reflect on my day. I closed my eyes and imagined myself six months into the future. I wore a black business dress with nude colored wedges and walked on to a brightly lit stage staring in the eyes of 1,000 kids. I clicked my remote and the slide presentation behind me displayed Ellen and I sitting across from each other at her studio. Next, I shared an image of Oprah and I speaking about education around the world in her beautiful home. For the first time to this audience, I revealed the picture behind me to show my book cover. I spoke into the microphone "Young Legends are you ready to be a game changer?"

After speaking for ten long minutes about how I crafted a brand around my advanced education journey, I left our leaders of a better tomorrow with a social media strategy. This helped them to reach 15,000 followers and drive traffic to their business or organization, plan to make their first $50,000, and provide inspiration to keep going. When I walked off the stage, I shook hands with the host and continued to the table to sell my book, course, and other products. A line clear to the back of the room stood in front of my table to meet A Young Legend.

I was able to meet almost everyone who had listened to me speak and inspired them to create their own version of success. They were able to ask me personal or professional questions to help them on their journey. I laughed, smiled, and took quite a camera full of pictures with the people who empowered me to stay on course. I was able to pass out information about dual enrollment and help them save money on college tuition to stay financially responsible.

Once I reached the last person, I sat down with a girl who followed me for a few years. She was at the TEDx event presented. She shared that I inspired her when I was on the TED stage. She went on to explain that she started a business that is now successful and allows her to travel the world with her family. I made sure to give her a big hug and thanked her for her support because she was one of my first audience members, subscribers, and Instagram followers. People like her are the reason why I love what I do. I walked back to the hotel room in New York City and began to remember that this was just a dream.

Before I knew it, my alarm went off and it was time to rise. I laid in the bed with my eyes wide open feeling satisfied of that dream. Every night I make sure to close my eyes with a dream I intend to visualize as my future. If I lay in bed from a very productive day, then I fall asleep to a short-term goal I plan to exercise. If I had a difficult day, I close my eyes to a long-term goal ten years from then.

Sometimes, I have unmotivated days and that is a time when I fall asleep to a dream about a mentor that I look up to. I usually imagine a grandfather that would lead me into his wonderfully crafted wooden library and show me all the literature that contributed to his family's success and happiness. He teaches me all the languages of the world because he values culture. He shows me things must create a successful life for myself. He is my visualization for showing me the right path on my business journey.

Manifestation is a great way to bring about opportunities in your life to help you achieve your goal. Dream visualization is a great way to fall asleep to positivity and what you hope for in your future. Sometimes it can comfort you when you had a challenging day and help you sleep with satisfaction because you are one day closer to success. It is difficult for me to find time during the day to visualize the goals I hope to achieve, so I added it into my nighttime routine after I say what I am grateful for. I usually lead my conversation with the universe by saying "Thank you for another wonderful day. I will wake up to a beautiful day." Then I follow with closing my eyes, breathing slowly, and choosing where I want to start my visualization journey to the future. Visualization is one great step toward manifesting your success because you fall asleep to where you see yourself in the future and wake up remembering the vivid dream you had about your version of success.

Chapter 3

Designing Your New Chapter

"You do not have to be great to start,

but you do have to start to be great."

- Zig Ziglar

My mother and I sat in the lobby looking at a book of my school's photography portfolio. In my left hand, I clutched my resume and proposal, scared that I would somehow ruin the freshly printed white papers. The assistant stepped away from her desk and motioned to me that he would be out soon. We had arrived on time and only waited a few minutes before the President of my College came outside of his office to shake my hand and usher me inside. We walked past the glass doors that stood ajar and I quickly glanced at myself. I wore one of my favorite blazer and pink pencil skirt, preparing to close this deal.

I had previously called the president's office almost one month earlier to schedule an appointment with him. I was attempting to prove to his assistant why I deserve to have a meeting with him, she interrupted me to say "Of course, of course. How is your grandmother?" I suddenly remembered that my grandmother worked there for over thirty years and I needed to thank her for helping me get this meeting. I hastily found a seat next to my mother in his well-decorated office, while he sat across from us. Sweat began dripping down my back, which is why I decided to wear a blazer. The last time the president and I met was at my grandmother's retirement party. He asked me a question regarding what school I attended, and I nervously answered with what grade I was in. Back to our meeting, we began talking about how classes were going until I initiated the conversation about how I can be more involved with the institution. I carefully handed him the papers that contained my resume and proposal along with three business cards to show why I wanted to be an ambassador to represent the dual enrollment student body.

As fast as I blurted my reason for scheduling an appointment with him, the gears in his head began turning. He began mentioning different ideas to implement this position and how I can participate and be more involved with the college. I left his office very hot and sweaty but ecstatic for the possibilities of my future at the school. Since then, I completed a six-month internship as an ambassador to include dual enrollment students in the college's activities, conferences, as well as resources to be a successful student achieving higher education.

I was not given an exact role within the student engagement and leadership department, but I eventually found my way. My beginning plan was to design a video series showing my experiences on campus as a dual enrollment student and providing great ways to be a successful teenage college student. Plans changed that did not allow me to fully pursue my idea because I was graduating soon, but I was able to be a representative for the school and share my story. I made great friends and connected with educational leaders while there, which I would not have been able to do unless I was interning. I was able to help create the Collegiate Leadership Conference along with the department. I made sure to include College Credit Plus students from all high schools in the area because it was available for all college students. During that time of reaching out to the schools and doing my best to include dual enrollment students, I felt that I achieved my set purpose at the Community College. It was also while hosting that event that I was given the chance to host a small workshop with my mother. We discussed "Financial Responsibility as an Agent of Change", which is where my theme was to help college students "take care of their home before impressing the streets." My mother spoke about buying a home and we answered questions to better assist the students in their individual situations. There were so many moments of satisfaction during that six-month period where my purpose in life evolved because I left room in my plan for such to happen. Many people were inspired by my story and wanted to take pictures with me because they felt that I would be an influential leader and businesswoman soon. My mother and I realized that people were really interested in my life and that I should figure out how to share it. I discovered that I cannot let my community down and they are expecting me to continue being great, changing the world, and building a generation better prepared for the future.

On the last day of my internship, I recorded a video with the social media marketing department regarding my intended topic, "College Credit Plus Student Survival Guide". Sadly, I was not able to achieve my set goal, but I accept other rewards that were unexpected and developed me into a better leader to help change the world. The video was my first attempt to talk about the things that are not mentioned with being a kid in college. I still plan to properly edit the video and share it with prospective and current dual enrollment students because it is useful information that I wish I would have known before I started. I was also asked to film my graduate story for their Facebook page to continue inspiring kids and adults to defy the walls built and become the pilot of their life. I finished the internship refreshed for the next chapter in life because just one month after, I graduated from high school and college and it was now my time to move on. One main chapter of my life had closed. I lived through two years of college, started my blog, and began sharing my story with my community. Following my double graduation, I was featured in the Columbus Dispatch for my achievement at sixteen years old and taking the initiative to encourage a program that could help solve the student debt crisis for future generations.

After I created my own position within the college, I noticed the connection my story and success had with a video I viewed. A human's mind filters many objects and thoughts when there are things that it should focus on instead. If someone is rushing to work to get to a meeting on time, they would not have noticed the bright red roses they passed on the way up to their office. As I was brainstorming ideas to share my story with education and business along with promoting dual enrollment for students to save on college tuition, one of the first opportunities that opened itself up to me was to start a blog. When you begin to live, breathe, and sleep your goal, you find ways to help you succeed.

I recalled my goals list of things I planned to accomplish in 2018. An easy way to help remind yourself to think and achieve projects for your plan is to write it on sticky notes and put it where you can read it. Like, when you wake up, brush your teeth, and wherever you eat. Make a reminder on your phone to notify you every day of affirmations, which are phrases to repeat and to manifest your future, such as "I am healthy, wealthy, full of joy" or "I am intelligent, a leader of my community, and a great social media influencer". I recommend creating Google alerts that can keep you updated on certain industries and people. They are daily emails regarding a keyword or phrase you would like found. I have google alerts for "business", "CEO", "billionaire", "royal family", and "dual enrollment" to help me provide the utmost value to my blog readers, in addition, to making me more knowledgeable about business. The plan that you create should be the main reminder you have and become obsessed to follow while allowing the journey to success develop you.

Make sure to not get caught up in how to start by only following the rules of business and what you should know before you start on your path. I was afraid to start all my various attempts at business because I felt that I had nothing to sell or provide to others. Yet, I have come so far developing my brand and business. Before I started on my blogging journey, I made sure to have written ten blog posts to publish. I left room to build quality content along the way, like my free ten step guide to graduate high school and college early when someone subscribes. I displayed a video of me speaking at TEDxNewAlbany and how to develop a plan and make the impossible possible. This was created even before I had a solid pitch for events and built a page on my website for booking me to speak later. Starting is always the hardest part of the journey to success, but it should not be the wall that blocks you from following your passion. Once you start, you will not regret the decision because it is only chapter one of your amazing existence on Earth.

Chapter 4

Pitch Punishment

"You've really got nothing to lose when following a
passion, but you do have everything to gain."
- Michelle Pierrot

Following Spanish class, I hurried to the next carrying my pink binder full of homework and graded assignments. I was passing what looked like an enormous group of eighth-grade students. I was thinking of the busy day ahead when one of my cheer friends walked by. I smiled and said hello when the words that came out of her mouth was not greeting me back. Suddenly, people seemed to close in a circle with us both. Someone who I had known for more than three years was standing in front of me with a look of the intent to harm. I always knew that she was mean to others, but we had our boundaries. Most of the students that I attended middle school with knew me as the "smart girl." She gazed down at my pearly white shoes that I had only worn one other time. I avoided wearing them for a good reason that I am sure you know as well, but they were very comfortable and matched my outfit that day. After she finished studying my shoes along with her friends, she asked the question that would be the first major turning point of my life, "Are those Nike's?" Seemed like a harmless question, right? If you had anything that looked like something it was not, you would not hear the end of it until your family moves away. While I sized up my new found enemy and spotted the different exits out of this makeshift boxing ring, I confidently said no. I walked to my next class, attempting to drown out the snickers, chuckling, and mean talk from people that I thought were my friends.

That ten-minute event felt like a day's affair. After I realized that I never wanted to feel that again, it was only the beginning. I stopped hanging out with those people. It only encouraged them because they continued with attacking every good thing I possessed. When eighth grade rolled around, I found a group where I wanted to belong. Me, myself, and I. I only wanted to experience other nice and positive people. It was difficult to break away, but something began to push me onto a path of greatness. I discovered business and the success mindset. I researched, and it became constant in my thoughts. My classmates grew tired of me regularly talking about business, but that was when I discovered that I was on the right track. I presented the last week of middle school on how to start a business and everyone began to see that I was not worried about the little things and I became respected.

Since middle school, it took me two additional years of high school to figure out the business that I wanted to kick off but, along the way I picked up knowledge for several other possible businesses. I had no idea then that I could see a future or knew that a business existed for being an influencer and blogger. My journey was not always easy and that remains, but I have since identified what I should do to keep improving my business. Blogging has been a way for me to inspire both parents and kids to try dual enrollment. It could change the lives of everyone who received a free college education. Each person who comments on my posts or fills out my contact form empowers me to continue my work. All the kids and parents who have confided in me for assistance with their educational journey was another source of satisfaction for me to keep pushing.

Since that day of being bullied, I made friendships that have groomed me into being a great leader and business person. The connections that I made with politicians, businessmen, and women, as well as social media influencers have all been because I shared my story with them. I would reach out to them to say I would love to connect with them.

I spent a summer attempting to craft a great essay to submit for a scholarship from Ellen DeGeneres and possibly be on her show. As soon as I pasted my 2,000-word essay into the essay box form, a red sentence below it revealed that I could only enter a certain number of characters. Unfortunately, I had to chop my beautifully written artwork in half to fit the requirement. It only took me two months to develop. I then added a great headshot and all my contact information. I submitted the document and waited six months to receive an email or letter in the mail inviting me to come on the show. NOTHING. Then, I filled out the form again giving her an update on my academic journey and sharing with Ellen that I would graduate soon. I repeated this process to contact Oprah as well. I am not sure Oprah or anyone that works with her received my email, but I was hoping we could meet to talk about dual enrollment because she is also involved in educational initiatives.

Make sure that you email people you want to meet and explain to them how you can provide value to a conversation. Although I have not been invited to be on the Ellen show and to meet Oprah, stay tuned. I am manifesting the opportunities to accomplish those goals and allow it to present itself to me. This will build my network to one day reach Ellen and Oprah.

A more successful story for me to share is when I emailed the director of College Credit Plus at the Ohio Department of Higher Education at midnight. I did not expect to receive an email the following morning, but I mentioned in the initial email that I had just graduated high school and college at sixteen years old in Ohio. I also mentioned that I wanted to stay updated on the success of College Credit Plus because I posted often about the program on my blog. After finishing off the email with "I would love to get a quick coffee with you," that call to action prompted a great response. Four months later, I sat down with the Director of College Credit Plus and we had a valuable conversation on how I can get more involved in my community to promote the underserved groups that may consider participating in the program. I was able to answer frequently asked questions for the director to design opportunities to collaborate with the Ohio Department of Higher Education.

A similar victory was achieved when I emailed a blogger and business owners thanking them for repinning my post or following my profile on Pinterest. At every chance I had, I was hitting send on my life story with the chance that a great opportunity would be delivered to my door. Believe it or not, I was given several guest post opportunities to help grow my blog audience and share my story on other influencer platforms. Now, people are writing about me and I only discover it when I Google myself.

While sitting in on an event, a group of kids came to speak to the host about entrepreneurship and Science, Technology, Engineering and Mathematics (S.T.E.M). They came in for lunch to receive insight about a day in the life. I introduced myself to the girls as a blogger and motivational speaker. After we dove into the conversation, I soon regretted not mentioning that I am a high school and college graduate at sixteen as well as a college student majoring in the field they were interested in hearing more about. As someone who encourages role models to create change for their community for minorities and women, I was not able to do so at that moment.

When the girls finished discussing their futures, I gave them my business card. I finally mentioned that I am an early graduate and teenage entrepreneur and suggested they check out my blog. They went to explore more when a family member of one arrived. I recognized them from an email I received a while before. I checked my email and my social media to see if they were the same people or knew of the people that had contacted me. I went up to the family to introduce myself and shook their hands. I looked at them saying, "I am A Young Legend from Instagram and I think you just emailed me." Their eyes lit up like the stars and the mother hugged me. She assumed that I lived in a different state when she contacted me the day before. We spoke for almost an hour about her son's success on a popular tv show, his business, and book. That Young Legend is amazing! I later met their daughter as their mother said, "this is the girl I was telling you about."

It really is a small world. I spoke to the family about their aspirations, goals, and how we could collaborate. "Sometimes you need people that look like you to show you the possibilities of life," their mother said. It shows you that life is endless with opportunities to create your own success. This moment is one I won't forget because it made me love my life purpose more than I did hours before. It was a pleasure to see a Young Legend that reached out to me through Instagram to feature them on my blog sitting beside me. It could not have gotten any better than that. The mother was so excited to see me because she was proud of my achievements even though we were strangers.

This was not the first time that I have made wonderful connections from unexpected events. I attended a local magazine steering meeting and went in with the expectation that I would hear about the direction of the publication. After listening closely, I found many people that I could see myself collaborating with. I made sure to pass my business card to the local food pantry to extend my services as a speaker and mentor. We connected briefly on ideas for the future. She was excited and said that I approached her at the perfect time. Next, I spoke to the magazine editor to let her know of stories I had written or scheduled to publish soon about Young Legends in the community. I again realized my purpose in the world continues to fall in place more and more with each person I make as a connection. Lastly, I was able to connect with the organizer of mom groups in nearby cities. I handed over my business card and asked what I could do to collaborate with their participating mothers. She mentioned knowing others who would love for me to speak to their children about my accomplishment. During a small one-hour event I was able to make lasting connections by taking the time listening closely.

That summer I was also present at a political event at a local country club. For more than one year I made a personal goal that I would go inside that exact country club. Sure enough, I ended up walking into what I envisioned for this event. All attendees were given the chance to listen to the republican and democratic side of candidates running for a specific congressional district for the state. I watched intently at the influential people of the city who frequented this country club as they sat around me. Important businessmen and women with important roles within the city were all standing in one room. I made sure to introduce myself to as many people as possible so that I could connect again at the next opportunity to see them around the community. This was not the right place to close a deal, but rather to introduce yourself to your community.

I paid close attention to the points that the politicians made, so that I could highlight that topic in the conversation I had with them later. I digested the information from both parties because I wanted to remain neutral. Both candidates supported dual enrollment, which I gladly mentioned while chatting with them. After all, I am an early graduate. I passed out my business card to those who seemed interested in my conversation and only introduced myself to those who did not seem very interested. Learn to get comfortable with the uncomfortable because you will be connecting with new people who could help your brand succeed.

Attend events that have nothing to do with your industry but have everything to do with entrepreneurship. I went to a healthcare information technology panel discussion and learned many lessons. From that event, I now know what the barriers to entry are when your clients are hospitals and athletic doctors. I understand the strategy I should take when trying to implement a product or service. I am aware of the method used to make sure your business is viable before wasting money on an idea. The entrepreneurs on the panel seats were sharing their stories that transformed from an idea to a profitable business. That experience was not specifically for healthcare startups, but for the innovators and industry disruptors who want to know how to take their business to the next level.

The power of networking is beyond measure when it comes to your future success. Speaking to people is both a learning and growing encounter. You have the potential to meet future friends, business partners, and mentors. Your network often reflects your net worth.

Another method to grow connections with people who will help you build up your brand is by direct messaging people on social media. Prior to creating an Instagram page, I had trouble finding teenage entrepreneurs to personally interview, feature on my blog, and reach out to inform them that I wrote a blog post about them. I can now promote their blog post feature on Instagram and let others know that I am always seeking to feature kids with a business. I follow various entrepreneurs, which I contact with the messaging capability to set up a time to highlight them and their endeavors. Many of the greatest blog stories of Young Legends that have accomplished amazing things despite their age has been found on social media with just a small audience. I find that makes for my perfect chance to share their story with my audience because every Young Legend needs their story told.

Iconic inventors, self-made business people, and influential leaders of the past and present all provide a roadmap for others to achieve the same level of success. I realized early on that others have studied the greats before them to know how to achieve their own version of success. You may have to make some adjustments to how you approach reinventing the wheel when starting your own business, but the path remains the same. Some achieve success by building a company in an industry that is quickly growing, like search engines and social media platforms. That is one way to becoming a billionaire because you are likely to grow at a swift rate utilizing the constant updates of technology and allow the public to invest and influence the future of the company.

If you ever create a business that you eventually sell to explore another business venture, you are more likely to gain financial wealth by being an avid investor. Warren Buffett and many others reached billions much later in life because their money grew with time, inflation, and the stock market. There are many great leaders to follow. You will find that you are not alone in your business journey to success. There are tremendous amounts of inspiring television shows, movies, and books that will help you to discover your role in the future of business.

Social media is the same with how you can achieve success as studying the greats. Social media can be compared to legendary people that provide the foundation for how you become an influencer. The articles of how to grow your following are like books of how to follow in the footsteps of an innovator. You may take a path to reach the same destination chosen but it takes a different turn to lead you there.

I have found several social media strategies that have repeatedly produced results for my brand and business. In the process of growing my audience on the platforms, I would find myself getting discouraged. I had no idea that I could drive traffic to my blog or get paid to speak at events across and out of the country from my efforts. I have found the best days and times that I should post on Instagram, and I continue to remain scheduled two weeks ahead of schedule. I've also found relevant content that I should promote on platforms such as LinkedIn, which I only discovered recently as a useful tool. I made sure to post content that I found would be useful on one platform versus another.

When I started my blog, I did not have social media and I am glad that I did not. I was still young, and I would not have used it to its full potential. I learned to grow my email list from word of mouth, media features, and simply passing out my business card. As soon as I made a business profile on Instagram, I made a strategy to post twice a day. I created a document that allows access from any device to quickly and easily comment hashtags to ensure it reaches new people. I was instantly able to connect with like-minded kids to feature and collaborate with, clients who booked me to speak, and people who can feature my story. I developed a strategy that has since made me money and will do so for you too!

You are an amazing entrepreneurial spirit. You have leverage over other business owners, social media influencers, and organization leaders. Your age does not matter. The story you must share with people is priceless but use it strategically. When you include your accomplishments, such as being a TEDx speaker, be sure to mention your business titles as chief executive officer or teenage entrepreneur and state your goal for the future to be a millionaire drop shipper or best-selling author. Your social media biography should be as intriguing as you are. Your news feed should reflect your ideas, goals, and knowledge as a thought leader of your community. When you attend an event for school, work, or business, capture those moments and share the lessons learned. This will show that you are a leader who values community, higher education or self-growth, and your amazing brand.

Begin to follow business leaders, upcoming entrepreneurs, and organization members to put your brand on their radar. If they appear smaller in impact, make sure to engage with likes and comments of how awesome their image appears or how amazing a project is that will change lives. Social media recognizes accounts that you have interest in for an event, organization, or potential feature platform. Comment saying "I would love to connect! You are doing amazing things." Next, lead into your story, "I am a seventeen-year-old entrepreneur and college graduate. I would love to collaborate." After I engaged with at least ten accounts, people began messaging me to jump on a conference call for a potential event or asked me to be featured in their magazine. If you are seeking opportunities to be featured, search the keyword "magazine." Look at the profiles that appear and engage with them. Instagram is a great way to show how you are impacting the world and spread your message.

LinkedIn is my newfound social media love because I can post business-related content and it will go beyond my immediate connections. I made an account my freshman year of high school for my business class and had not referred to it until recently. I had sixteen connections on LinkedIn when I posted my vlog "A Day in The Life of a College Graduate At 16 Years Old". It has since gained over 400 views and still growing. Many people have contacted me through the messaging capability on LinkedIn to speak to their organization or be involved with an upcoming project. It has also been a great way for me to connect with people that I reach out to feature me or to speak at their event. This allows them to stay updated on my professional journey. My blog posts have also been shared beyond my connections. This a great way for your story to be shared outside of your followers on Instagram and email list. I connect with people on LinkedIn that I believe are doing great work in the community and I could collaborate with. If someone is the founder and president of an organization, I contact them to see how I can be involved with their mission.

When you build consistency in your business, you can easily find the strengths and weaknesses of your strategy. At one point I would only release my blog post on my website for the small amount of organic traffic I had that may stumble upon it, but eventually, I built an email list to suggest my content for subscribers to read. But, if I send an email for a post to my subscribers on another day or time, my open-rate and click through rate decrease dramatically. When I became dependable, my audience knew when to engage with my content. I post on Instagram every weekday at the same time every morning and evening. When I became intentional in when I wanted my audience to view new content, my followers could begin to predict when to look for my images. The same goes for several other items in my business. I have constructed a plan of action that allows me to leave room for creativity while I build a successful business and provide a space for my audience to be an engaged community.

I attended a design event that was centered around growing your social media audience and monetizing. Any time that I am present at an event, I dress in business attire. You never know who you could meet. I began to make a long walk to the building. I soon realized that I should not have worn a dress and wedges because I was immediately hit with a steep flight of stairs. I journeyed up the dark hallway and creaky floors. I turned the hall a few times before I heard the noise of a large group of people. I walked into the room and instantly felt overwhelmed with beautiful views of my city. The large office space was renovated compared to the rest of the building. I found a small bench to sit on and began listening to catch up on what I missed. Listening intently to the conversation I realized the people surrounding me were all designers. They were all creatives and artists attempting to build a business by leveraging social media. Those that hosted the event were large social media influencers with 15,000 - 200,000 followers on Instagram alone. They started their discussions by telling stories and allowing others to ask questions that would lead into a group conversation.

People began expressing how overwhelming it can be making a strategy that leaves room for creativity but also brings in clients and revenue. Someone then recommended a free scheduling tool, which I currently use. Another person mentioned that using a scheduling tool can work against you because it recognizes the use of third-party programs rather than organic posts from its users. That is why I have the program notify me that I need to post at a certain time, so it transfers my picture, I paste in my caption, and use hashtags from a document on my phone to comment thirty for maximum exposure. As we transferred to the topic of hashtags, one man shared a great strategy to only use hashtags with between 5,000 and 30,000 posts. Hashtags below that aren't used often enough and hashtags above are used too often and limits growth and exposure.

Although, I agree majority of them should be within that guideline, I noticed that when I used more common hashtags, I receive more engagement on those posts than those with a smaller hashtag. A friend of the host is an artist and she began telling her story. She plans out her posts two months in advance, yet she leaves one day each week to post her thoughts for the day.

The last story told before we left from the charming, white loft was about a girl who used to make designs for a well-known company. When she began putting her work on social media, it went viral. She had one billion likes and millions of downloads of her content, until people began using her designs for negative use. She eventually had to start over on social media and never included her face, so her work would remain anonymous. Because of the unfavorable events that happened in her life due to social media, she stated one thing that impacted every person in the room. Although she has 200,000 plus followers, she only has 500 people from social media that pays her bills. Once she realized that, she focused her efforts on the small community that has been with her from the beginning and supports her as an artist.

The lesson to take from this, the numbers are great when it comes to building a business where you can leverage social media to make an income, but it should never be your main focus. Having a large following may not mean that everyone will like your posts, comment, or purchase your product. The people who really matter are the people who have watched you grow, are happy to share your content, and support the brand you are trying to get out to the world. Never forget about those who have been with you from the beginning and will continue to support you on your journey to success.

Moments I attend motivating events like this, ignite my passion for my purpose to inspire others again. Often my mother must put me on "Pitch Punishment." I am always scouting for kids to send a message or sharing my story at events where I could possibly speak. I absolutely love every minute of hitting send on my life story because I inspire so many people to keep going on their journey to success. Sometimes I will spend days and several hours pitching people with the intent of spreading my message and building my network to eventually create my net worth. While in middle school where the world seemed to be against me, was a turning point in my life to travel a different path and connect with people who will only make me a better person.

Chapter 5

No Class Reunion

"You've got what it takes,
but it will take everything you've got."
- Unknown

I walked past the tall, white pillars that seemed to be holding the brick building together. I opened the front doors of my high school and began to walk towards the lobby. I pushed the next set of large doors to find two desks on either side of the room. I had a very important appointment to be presented my high school diploma by the principal. Unfortunately, I would not be walking across the stage at my future graduation ceremony. I waited on the wooden bench until everyone who contributed to my official graduation entered the room.

The brief moment of accepting my diploma and shaking hands with the principal flew by, but we did take a moment for my mother to get a picture of us. I shook with my right hand and held my diploma in the left. I was presented my unofficial diploma

December of 2017, though I would not otherwise receive it until May of 2018 when the rest of the class would later graduate. I transferred to a college out of state, but I was sure to receive my certificate of completion before I left. Months later I received the official college diploma in the mail.

I was not aware that the principal would be presenting my diploma to me that day, but I was grateful that he did. I put a great amount of work into accomplishing what I set forth two years before that moment, and I would miss the proper ceremony that all the other students would receive months later. My story of how I received my recognition sums up the obstacles I faced to reach that lobby and stand next to the principal.

The moment I had to glance down at my protected certificate of completion of high school made me realize that I achieved this at sixteen years old and everyone else can do the same. I had given my business card to the Principal before, but I had a feeling that I would be back very soon. Now, I can go back to speak to my high school to share how I completed it. The students can have someone to tell them they can do anything they set their mind to with real results.

The film that covered my signed, dated, and glossy document was the beginning of my journey to academic and business success. I would not have a successful business today unless I had continued with the path to graduate early. I had several complications with my high school and college communicating with each other about my advanced plan. I jumped through unimaginable hoops to hold that small book carrying my diploma.

It represented all the possibilities of when a kid develops a plan. When I walked out of the brick building, passing the beautifully mowed lawn, and through the black iron gates, that would be the last time I attended New Albany High School.

As I walked to my car, students began scurrying to their next class. It was then that I realized once again I will not attend homecoming, prom, senior brunch, or the graduation ceremony. I sacrificed those events that were made important to me when I was younger but to find my passion in learning, business, and speaking. I made choices for my future that I will never regret, but I will be in a very different stage of my life than others.

I once watched an Olympic athlete that was on my local news channel. She explained that she missed a great amount of school activities because she was always training and doing what she loved. She also stated that she has moments of wondering "what if" but does not dwell too long for she is on a journey that she enjoys every moment. That story resonated with me. It was like she was speaking to me. She was telling me that the things people said were important to teenagers are not all they are cracked up to be. It can be a distraction from what is important. I think that is the one thing I realized early on, the shoes, clothes, and latest phone are not all that valuable if you do not have a great job to help you afford those things. Live a life like others won't, so you can live a life like others can't. Your future self will thank you for the sacrifices you made to be financially responsible, dedicated, and a great role model for others.

Make sure to only make choices that will help you meet your end goal. My sophomore year of high school I auditioned for the school cheerleading team. Sadly, I did not get on the team, but eventually, I recognized that I should be grateful for the rejection. If I made the team, I probably would not have graduated from school as early as I did and would not have had time to start my blog. I would have been juggling much more on my plate and would not have focused as much on my education as I did.

I recommend leaving room in your life for those unscripted moments where you try new interests, but if you don't succeed try to understand why it was best to not have. You will have moments where your focus should be so intense that others think you are crazy. If you find that you have a great opportunity, do not jump to immediate conclusions. I attended investment club at my high school every Wednesday because that was an industry I wanted to learn. I love the stock market and I gained a large amount of knowledge and insight about how to invest your money and make more of it. The leaders of that group started investing in penny stocks and it gave me great opportunities to network with other teenage entrepreneurs with business mindsets. I even decided to be investment leader the following year but had to step down due to my college load and that I would be graduating in the middle of the school year.

I was given the opportunity to learn an industry, which I had plans to explore once I became profitable. I discovered that I love the idea of investing with the intent of passively growing my money. If I ever decided to get a job with my future computer

44

science degree, I would explore financial company positions. I absolutely enjoy the possibilities to grow and control your money, even though trading on the stock market is crazy.

I passed on good opportunities to take better chances for my education and business success. I only enrolled in one class at my high school, so I will probably not attend my class reunion, but I will be able to say that I have spoken to schools across the country sharing my story of receiving my high school diploma only ten days prior to walking across the stage to be presented my college degree. My school journey was not all that bad. I was very fortunate to attend my graduation ceremony at my local community college. Moments like that where you are greatly recognized for all the hard work you have done, be sure to pat yourself on the back. Spend time with the people who helped you get to that moment because they worked just as hard and more for you to succeed. No class reunion, but I am a high school and college graduate at sixteen, and I run my own business.

Chapter 6

Rejection Leads to Success

"Rejection tests whether you are

serious about your dreams"

- Unknown

I watched the "Back to the Future" movie series and instantly came up with an idea that could transform the world's energy source into renewable energy. If you have not watched the movie, I highly recommend it because the series will get your brain stirring about the possibilities of life. Back to the Future is about a scientist who builds a car that travels to the past and future alongside an adventurous kid that follows the scientists on his adventures. The scientist, Doc, comes back from the future with a souped-up car that has Mr. Fusion attached. Mr. Fusion converts aluminum, banana peels, and much more into energy for the iconic car to operate. That moment of inspiration eventually led to an amazing senior project.

The next day after binge-watching the three-part movie series, that concept continued to sit with me almost as if I had the next big thing. Eventually, I started the conversation with myself about what other things could be converted into energy. As I was researching the fantasy Mr. Fusion, which has its own fan page, I ran across human and animal secretion that can convert into energy. That discovery launched five months of research, conception, and design, which I can now say is a 3-D design. After I found a problem to solve and grow a global business, I decided to use the idea formed for a senior project. I had the opportunity to complete a project that I was passionate about and spend one hundred hours of my summer dedicated to something that I wanted to see on paper. I was determined to find out if it was a real business idea.

Just a few weeks before school was out and I would have to start my project, I was tasked to find a highly educated mentor to help me along the way. I called the local chamber of commerce after uncovering a successful mentorship program they offered. I made the decision to finally call and the person I spoke to mentioned a company that would be perfect for support that I needed. I eventually contacted the business, which had great scientists and a lab for me to use for my project. An executive for the company tried to find a scientist who would be able to dedicate a certain amount of time to help me accomplish the plan for my project. Unfortunately, I did not move forward because I found another excellent mentor that was difficult to find.

I finally decided to contact the local university where other students had successfully found mentors. My investment leader discovered his first business invention during his senior project with the help of his mentor. That was the story that empowered me to find a lifelong mentor to help take this movie idea to a school project to a boardroom invention. After long hours on the phone, I reached an important lady in the chemical engineering department. She spent a few weeks searching for a professor that had enough time to coach me on how to build a very scientific product that dealt with complicated gases.

I spoke on the phone at her request with five scientists, four of which told me I cannot do what I set out to do. My first real experience with rejection was when I planned a conference call with a professor who had experience with my topic, anaerobic digestion. He blatantly stated that I did not have enough time, enough materials, or the right idea to make it possible. He said that it was "nearly impossible" to build a product that converts household waste into natural gas for cars in one summer.

I journeyed through three other chemical engineering scientists that proceeded to tell me the same, but I did not give up. Ever since I had this tremendous idea that could change the world, nothing could stop me, including a few educated scientists. I had dreams and visions of the world being a better place because energy was made from the landfills that clog up our land, turning what is considered useless into an empire. I ultimately spoke to a professor in the Chemical and Biomolecular Engineering department. I enjoyed my time spent with him because he joined my project with the intent of helping me design something that can be attainable for the everyday family to afford. He was the mentor who believed in me and could help me translate my idea into a workable product.

Three months of a one hundred plus hour project in addition to three college classes in one summer was difficult to juggle, but I would not have change a thing. I now know that my product is achievable, although the world is not ready for a concept like that.

From a business perspective, there aren't enough natural gas cars or enough people purchasing natural gas cars for my product to reach the market yet. I still have the 3-D design on my laptop and I think about it often because I still brainstorm other ideas to change the world by making the purpose of my product work with a largescale plan. Stay tuned!

I was able to present my findings, research, and 3-D design with my high school teachers and other students. My mentor and family also attended, which meant a lot to me because other students did not have the same support. I presented my product to the senior class and told them a great way to help make the world a better place for the next generation of game-changers because we deserve to treat the world as we treat our family, priceless!

My first occurrence with major rejection was not my last, but each time I have prevailed and succeeded ten times better than others said I could. When I first found out about dual enrollment and the opportunities provided to take free college classes, I attempted to register for the program. I ran into many roadblocks along the way just to receive advisement on how to get started with a new program for students as young as in seventh grade to replace their current classes and receive dual credit. People told me that "this program really was not designed for students like you" because I was too young to take on college classes. Now that I have graduated high school and college at the ripe young age of sixteen years old, I can say they were wrong. I even faced rejection to graduate because of one class that I was unaware would not apply to what I needed to receive my Associate of Science degree.

Never let rejection stop you from following your dream. Never. You are more than capable of pushing through those challenging times and I am a living testimonial to that. Sometimes rejection is just a way of checking if you are following your true passion and if you are ready to see success. The rainbow does not come until after the storm has passed and success is the same way. The athletes, actors, and social media influencers that you look up to would not be able to live in that big mansion if they did not work as a waitress at night while they are paying for classes and equipment. All the social media platforms that you use for your entertainment would not be so popular if the chief executive officer did not spend long nights programming while attending classes at an ivy league college or living in their parent's basement.

The universe does not want you to waste your time doing something if you have not prepared to enter and survive the storm. You are more than capable of making it to see the rainbow, but you must be willing to be the only person who believes in yourself for a while. Sometimes you may have a great friend or family member who believes in you so much that you keep you going through the brick walls that may stand in your way to success. But, they would not do so if they did not see your potential greatness. It is a pivotal moment when my mom said that she wishes she had a friend like me when she was younger to motivate her.

If you do not have a great support system, be your own mentor. Stand in the mirror and say the things your mentor would say to you to prepare you for a hard test. Read the books that your mentor would encourage you to read and dress the way you would expect if you were where you wanted to be. Find quotes that will help to maintain your motivation to keep creating and collaborate with people who are on the same level as your mentor and where you eventually hope to be. You are capable of greatness and never forget that because you will tell the next person who looks up to you for direction and inspiration. I once thought about quitting, then I noticed who was watching, younger students, little cousins, and an audience of driven kids.

Chapter 7

Gathering Seeds for Your New Lifestyle

"When you want to succeed as bad as you want to breathe, then you will be successful."

- Eric Thomas

In school my class was assigned a career management discovery project. I presented my career and salary to my eighth-grade class. I demonstrated what my life would be like as an adult in the project manager profession with a salary of roughly $32,000. The classmates following my presentation explained their careers of music producers, dancers, and athletes. The last presenter stood in front and illustrated her career as an anesthesiologist with a salary of $400,000. That moment was the first of many wake-up calls to encourage me to follow a different path.

During that same school year, I discovered the subject business and the possibilities when you follow your passion.

Sometimes the environment that you are in influences your life decisions. If you had never met someone that was a social media influencer, motivational speaker, or real estate developer, you would think that the most valuable career is a nurse. Most students that I knew of were under the impression that a nursing profession is the highest paid opportunity. During that time, I realized what I had been taught in school was a small fish in a large pond full of possibilities. I had never seen a house that was worth $1,000,000 and when I did I had no idea that those existed in my state where doctors, lawyers, and business owners lived.

Glass ceilings are imaginary boundaries that have been placed on certain people that have power over our thoughts in education, business, and finance. When you discover another world of chances for success, never forget it. That is your little chance to break the brick wall that has separated you from higher education classes, clubs in school that teach you how to invest in the stock market, and small businesses that you can start as a teen to create future freedom.

The entire duration of my sixth-grade school year, I envisioned the moment of my teacher presenting the beginning of our class assignment. I sat at my desk in the front row with my foggy glasses not allowing me to sit any further away from the board to see properly. I watched the other students begin to file into their seats around me. The bright morning light appeared as spring began to creep into the sleep left remaining in our eyes. My science teacher strolled into the lab-focused classroom and stood behind her large desk to write on the board words pertaining to the exciting day we all dreamt about the night before. In red writing, the phrase "College Day" appeared.

My teacher turned around to face the blaring sunlight of the rows of large windows in the science room and smiled at her excited students. She then tasked us all to begin searching for a college we would like to attend based on our dream careers. Everyone waited impatiently to grab their Chromebook provided by the STEM school and begin their research. She continued to explain that we would contact our universities, with the intent to receive materials representing our selected school and would be displayed in the hallway. I later noticed that the small billboard on the school's cement wall carried the college memorabilia of the previous year's sixth grade students.

Once all the students were finally given the chance to work on their individual projects, I already knew where to start. I began looking for colleges that specialized in performing arts and stumbled upon University of California Los Angeles (UCLA). I narrowed down to outstanding dance schools, which also led me to UCLA. I spent the remaining day in my science class researching the opportunities offered for my future position.

I had been dancing for two years leading up until that exact moment of finding a school to continue my then passion. I loved hip-hop and ballet, but absolutely enjoyed lyrical. Dance was a great way to express my feeling through body movements, especially to music that I connected with. I was ecstatic to advance my findings in an extracurricular I enjoyed, like most other dancers at my school that attended the same local studio.

Weeks later when I finished my project, I contacted the university. They never sent me information or branded products to display, but that was my opportunity to think about my future before it crept up on me. I began to take notice of the numbers I should pay attention to. I now realize that I was attempting to attend a school in a very expensive city, but I aspired to follow through on being a professional dancer. I took heed to the level of dance I would need to obtain as well as the application process as a performing art major.

This project was not the first time that I had thought about college early. My mother started the conversation with me in third grade. We were in the car headed to visit my grandmother at work. The discussion began with what to expect in college. As we pulled up in a parking space in front of the school where she worked, my mother expanded on the different careers. I realize now that was one of the most valuable conversations we had early in my life. That is what allowed me to know what I wanted in sixth grade. Before I knew much about middle school, I was aware of the possibilities of college. She took precious time to prepare me for the future because it was necessary for success.

Looking back, that is the best time to start many conversations about life. College is a big decision, especially when the cost is tacked on because it can change the course of your life. My mother prepared for my education before I valued the time I spent in class and paid attention to the books I read. It is never too early to start making your own success.

I was the only one at my school that capitalized on the dual enrollment program to pay for majority of my college classes, providing the chance to graduate early. I was dedicated to taking free college classes so much that I enrolled in classes on Saturdays. Each Saturday I had classes from eight in the morning until two in the afternoon as well as managing online classes. During that semester I woke up tired but committed as I passed every house where people were still sleeping in their warm beds. My mother took me to college when the rest of the world was dark and recovering from their long week. I can proudly say that every decision and sacrifice I made to graduate on time was well worth it. My life has drastically changed allowing me to inspire men, women, and children while making an income.

To continue shattering the glass ceiling set above me, I leave room in my life for personal growth. I attend conferences, summits, and workshops because I want to stay updated on my business and industry. The chamber of commerce for cities and innovative organizations have events to provide resident's free information. Reading books are the most convenient and affordable options to gain knowledge about anything ever desired. You can grab a copy of *Think and Grow Rich by Napoleon Hill*, which explains the thirteen principles to make whatever amount of money you desire. *Rise and Grind* by Daymond John, an investor shark on *Shark Tank*, and *Our Kind of People: Inside America's Black Upper Class* by Lawrence Otis Graham are also both insightful reads. Everything is at your fingertips, you just must look carefully. Google Alerts will email you daily articles to administer information, so you can stay updated. YouTube can give tips to grow your Instagram profile to 10,000 followers to start making income from sponsorships and affiliate products or teach you how to program for your future web development company. Mentors are one direct message away. Your Instagram gives you constant awareness into the lives of social media influencers, politicians, and business leaders to know their daily habits and projects to be the next Forbes cover. What are you waiting for?

On Fridays, I designate a time to work on content creation for the future and evolution of my business. Create a consistent time for you to work on the business tasks or courses you have been waiting to dive into. This will eventually help you designate when you are most productive to push out content for brand building. I understand that this might also be a time when you want to hang out with friends, but what is more important for your future success? I sacrificed my Saturdays, so I could graduate early and start college classes that apply to my major in Computer Science early and travel the country speaking to people like you. I worked until mid-afternoon, then went to the office to work on my business until late at night. On the weekend, I worked all day to produce YouTube videos, Instagram posts, and blog posts. I have spent time creating products and services where I can make the most money for as little time as possible.

I am regularly thinking of methods to grow my brand and more sources of autopilot income. Being comfortable with the uncomfortable will allow you try new areas within your brand. Attend networking events, so that you can build your network. You might just find a magazine that is interested in featuring a young entrepreneur. I pitched an organizer with the intent of speaking at her event and she asked to interview me for her podcast. The second kid I interviewed on my blog emailed me to ask permission to use my article in a magazine feature. Next thing I know, the owner of *Desh Videsh* magazine is on the phone with me to use my entire article as her feature and highlighted me with a picture and bio as the author in the Indian-American magazine.

I have owned my domain name and managed my blog for over one year and counting. Now, I have subscribers coming from all over the country and being featured left and right. The nights that I stayed up late or spent my weekends working are paying off. I now travel across the country, soon around the world, and this is only the beginning. Again, what are you waiting for? I would not have had an enticing topic to speak about on the TEDx stage if I had not spent two years, non-stop, attending college classes to graduate high school and college at sixteen years old. I would not have a title of seventeen-year-old entrepreneur, blogger, and motivational speaker if I was not writing blog posts when no-one was reading them. I am here to tell you to just do it. You must start to eventually see the success but enjoy the journey along the way. I would not have a book to write if I did not work more than forty hours a week doing what I love. You have potential for greatness and you must believe it because I started out like you.

Now I fall asleep dreaming of my success. I have pictures on my phone and laptop of the house I want to live in and the person I see myself transforming into. I have affirmations that I speak each morning and every sense of gratitude I possess I review in my mind while I am in the shower. I have days of reflection as I write when I never thought I would be in the business of storytelling through my fingers, then evolving into my words. When you spend every moment with the desire to succeed, trust me when I say, "it will come your way".

Chapter 8

Give Your Audience Something to Buy a Ticket For

"The person who does more than they are paid for will soon be paid for more than they do."

- Napoleon Hill

At the very beginning of my business journey, I started out with only three subscribers, my mother, my grandmother, and myself. I will never forget how I built my email list and still growing. Then, I was creating three blog posts a week and loved every minute of it. Suddenly, I lost the passion because I did not have a large enough audience to satisfy my drive. I worked hard to comment and create guest posts on other blogs to grow my audience. Eventually, kids and parents started to reach out to me through my blog because they saw a comment I made under a dual enrollment blog and wanted advice. They wanted to know more about how I graduated early and what classes they should enroll in to get on the same track.

I can guarantee that if you continue to put out great value and work hard to grow your audience, eventually you will have an audience larger than your dreams. You can never give up because if you do, you will never see the success of your hard work. You may not know it based on your Analytics data, but you are changing lives. You are inspiring your parents to keep going because they have a child motivating others to follow their dream. Your family members look up to you and see their potential success when they work hard. Would you quit if you knew who was watching?

I started my series of blog posts about kids called Young Legends, where I share stories of kids achieving something extraordinary despite their age. I've always wanted to create a platform for like-minded children to build a network of other entrepreneurs and game changers. Before I was able to contact accomplished people or be in the company of that type of person, I wrote blog posts about them from articles I found. Now, I use Instagram as a platform to discover the next Bill Gates all around the country.

Everyone must start somewhere, so do not let the first step to success stop you. You can create a free website and purchase a $0.99 domain name. Use your website as a platform for any business you would like to start. You can design and purchase business cards from OfficeMax or Staples for $20.00 so that people begin to take you seriously. If you do not have the money to do that, start making videos to upload to YouTube or Instagram. Technology is at your fingertips and you underestimate your phone.

If you would like to grow your Instagram to one be a social media influencer, you'll need at least 10,000 followers for other brands to consider you for endorsements. Post pictures two to three times per day with great hashtags. If you want to be a speaker, reach out to local organizations and volunteer to speak to the youth. Make sure to have someone record video of your speech, so that you can begin making a profit after a few speeches. You will find that people will offer to pay you for your hard work. You have an advantage over all other entrepreneurs, use it!

News media outlets, newspapers, magazines, and social media influencers are looking for people like you to promote. You are easily able to write a book and sell out of the stores. You can make money because you are giving back to the community while you are in high school. You are doing amazing things and people are happy to share your story with the world.

One day I saw an old classmate. She was dressed on one end of the career spectrum and I was leaning towards the other. I reflected on how much money I was able to profit in speaking for thirty-minute comparing it to what many may make working several hours each week. I share this, to challenge you to expand on not what you do, but how you can be valued in making the most for your time. Believe or not, that person used to make fun of me for valuing my education, not having social media, and being interested in business.

I speak to kids and adults about how to develop a successful plan to make the impossible possible and start building a brand. I share value every time I go onto the stage. If you feel that you do not have value to provide just yet, read the information you are interested in and put it to the test. If you want to talk about marketing or social media, create a social media page and use the steps you read to create a successful method. Finally, you have something to talk about, content to write a book, and a method to make an income. It is just that easy.

If you want to create a product, sample it as a school project. Plunge into that area and spend your time becoming obsessed about your idea. Eat, sleep, and breathe it all because you want to know your facts backward and forward. You can create a challenge to share your progress with others in your community and possibly launch a crowdfunding site to get your business started. If you want to start a service business, provide expertise to family members or community leaders for free and ask for testimonials and referrals. Vlog about the case studies you are currently working on and give your feedback on the success and failures. Ask to shadow someone in the Mayor's office of your city and listen very closely. Find out where you want to be and ask them a couple of questions. You are amazing, and people recognize when you have the potential for greatness and willing to work for it.

I love emailing people and writing blog posts, enough to spend the entire day working on that alone. Time seems to fly by, but I am thrilled to be the pilot of my own journey. I have come a long way from a beginner website and 100-word diaries about my challenges with dual enrollment. I started with reaching out to my college president and during that time I did my first workshop. I had no idea that I wanted to be a speaker. I then connected with the director of dual enrollment at the department of higher education in my state. I manifested the opportunity to do a TEDx Talk, just from an open mic night audition, which lead to being offered a paid internship based on my branding work. Now I travel the country as a teenage entrepreneur, college graduate, motivational speaker, and author. The possibilities are endless for your success.

As the host of a summit began to quiet down the room to kick of the morning, I was signaled to begin walking towards the stage. She grabbed the microphone and told the kids about what to expect for the day, including me a seventeen-year-old speaker. She introduced me as high school and college graduate at sixteen years old that had reached out to her to get involved. As my website was pulled on the projector, the page halted on "About A Young Legend." I was handed the microphone and began sharing my journey to the middle of the stage.

At my first paid speaking engagement, I was not sure how the high school audience would react. I was reminded of how cool kids may seem, so I was nervous to show my true colors. I started the speech by introducing myself and everything seemed to fall into place. Again, I felt that this was my true calling beyond blogging. I was changing lives through my words, which transformed me into a powerful force to be reckon within five seconds.

That day, I left the kids with three steps to a successful plan and three easy steps for them to start building a brand for whatever career they choose to go into. I finished off my ten minutes of inspiration with time for questions, to allow space for individual connections to form. My mother was then called up to the stage to be interviewed about how she contributed greatly to my success. She discussed with the parents attending that wanted to help set their kids up for success with technology, business, and education. We left the stage empowered to make a difference because I was reminded that my generation is amazing. The kids asked many questions about time management, social media, and branding, to a point where I regretted ever assuming they would not be interested in what I had to say.

My mother and I were thanked for our time and we headed to our table in the back of the room for the planned day to continue. I sat in my seat and my mother began to dismantle the camera and tripod. The organizer of the event started a recap discussion with the attendees to talk about the points the kids found interesting. Several kids raised their hand to share notes they had taken, I was amazed. They remembered quotes I used to guide the direction of my speech and understand that they can do anything they dreamed and worked towards. At that moment I almost forgot that I was their age. I would have been a junior in high school, just like them. I then realized that was my competitive edge compared to other speakers and adults is that I am someone exactly like them telling them anything is possible.

After the other speakers finished up their presentations about being professional on social media and encouraging students to explore STEM majors, a line formed in front of my table. The students were let loose to explore the career expo part of the summit. Parents came up to hear more information from my mother about "how she did it" and how I could further their kid's journey to success. Some of the kids who attended the event alone, came up to thank me for speaking to them and congratulate me on my achievements. I walked out of the building where the event was held with pure joy because I watched lives be impacted right before my eyes. I knew this was my calling.

Before I left the stage, I told the kids about an exclusive giveaway I was hosting just for attendees of that event. They entered in a giveaway one by one, and I saw wonder and mystery settled on their faces. What could a seventeen-year-old entrepreneur be giving away? One month later I chose a winner that I believe was well deserving. When I emailed the winner to tell him the good news, I am sure text could not properly display his emotions to me. I sent a package with two gift cards, a one-year subscription to Entrepreneur magazine, and a personal thank you card. That was an amazing moment in my life because I was able to impact a kid outside of being on a stage and extend another part of my service to be a mentor if they ever need one. I am here because of them.

The following month I spoke at a local organization. It was a smaller audience with younger kids, but the impact was the same. I was nervous for this day because the age of the audience. The lesson learned is never underestimate the smart minds of our generation. The environment was different as the kids sat on the floor of a room and I stood above. After my ten minutes of speaking, the kids flooded me with great questions about dual enrollment.

Later we all took a picture and I passed out business cards to each kid. As I was thinking the person who encouraged me to speak to this amazing group, one girl motioned for me to come over. She whispered that she had a personal question and went on to ask what she should do if she has test anxiety. I quietly told her, to not make her feel embarrassed to ask a great question like that, "say in your mind, "winners never quit, and quitters never win."

As my college classes became more difficult, I sometimes cried because I did not know the answers. As a graduate, I now know that because I never gave up and pushed through the hard tests, studying for longer hours than I did in high school, the time I put in was rewarded with a college degree. That same quote stayed closely with me after a transformational and international speaker, said the quote on a video recording of a speaking engagement from years ago. The story that the speaker paired with that inspiring quote proved the success she had as a younger swimmer. I will never forget it and I hope the girl I shared it with does the same.

Don't wait to start because you are only pushing back your success. You never know who is watching. When you achieve the success you have been looking for and even along the way, make sure to thank those who contributed to your accomplishments. Sometimes I forget how much others have sacrificed for me to travel. My family purchased my domain name and business cards while keeping the lights on. The edited my blog posts and listened to me as I practiced my speeches. Other people like your family, teachers, mentors, and friends are your lifeline. Some people may not believe in you, but if they paid for your Starbucks to meet a potential client, then they deserve a thank you.

You are a Young Legend full of promise. You now have the steps of The Strategic Mind of A Young Legend" that allowed me to graduate early and build a successful brand the changes the world one word at a time.

"Every Young Legend Started out with a
Dream to be Legendary."
- Amara Leggett

Final Words

Desire is what you hope to achieve in the world. Inspire is how you influence the next generation to achieve their desire. You have two roles in the world to be the student, then the teacher. You never know what you can be until you believe and what you can achieve until you write it down. Tomorrow you could discover another path to explore on your journey. I always keep my mind wide open to the possibilities as should you. When you begin to walk the yellow brick road, remember the lessons learned along the way. Your best teacher is your last mistake. Make sure to share your mistakes with the world because you would wish that someone else would do the same when pursuing a place that is less traveled. You are a good leader when you mentor others to be a leader too. Here are my biggest realizations of pure happiness for my set purpose, to inspire others to accomplish success.

Gratitude Brings More Your Way

Having gratitude for what you possess each day, helps you enjoy what sits in front of you. Remember that not everyone has what you have. You may not believe that you are privileged when you experience obstacles but continue to fight for what you know to be true about yourself. Take time to look out the window and appreciate the elements that helps you survive. Say thank you aloud for your arms, legs, and ability to move. Feel happiness for the internet, your cell phone plan, and other materials that allow you to build your empire. You are carrying out the plan to attain your desire but are you grateful for what you have now for that you desire.

The Law of Attraction Works

We are energy. What you are reading is energy. Your feelings, dreams, and beliefs are energy. The world is made up of energy and it cannot be created nor destroyed. What you manifest out into the world will come full circle and back around. Believe what you want to come true like more opportunities for your brand to grow. Belief is so strong, that miracles can happen. Many people have defied the laws set before them and they contribute their success to dedication, becoming obsessed, and the belief. The law that you can attract what you desire is only so if you believe it to be. Negativity can diminish the progress you have put out into the world, so stay focused.

Plan Your Success

Developing a plan to make a certain amount of money each year is hard to grasp when you have no idea how may deals you need to close each day, week, and month. Breaking down the details of your goal, makes it seem more attainable because you know exactly what you must accomplish. Write your goal on paper and put it where you will be able to see it each day like by your bed, on the bathroom mirror, and definitely as a morning reminder on your phone. You will notice that you are always thinking about your desire and are often finding ways to bring about more than you planned. As you write your goal, practice visualizing what feeling you will have when you achieve it. Imagine the smell of your restaurant, sound of the beach waves, and the feeling of an animal's fur when you heal their wounds. Conceptualize the freedom you will have as a result of following your passion. As you write the words that form phrases of your goals, trust that you will prosper.

You Have the Potential for Greatness

Greatness means something different to many people, but to me *Impact* and *Legacy* come to mind. Find out what your version of greatness is, then make it your true end goal. This can be something that will take your lifetime to grasp in your hand, or longer. We are all here for a reason, so find your purpose. You may discover what your greatness is after you experience the success you envisioned. Success does not end once you purchase the home, business, or car of your dreams. Success is that you transformed your passion into your purpose. Plan for your desire, which is a short-term goal, to align with your greatness, that lasts forever.

Never Let Your Situation Determine Your Success

One idea that resonated closely with me is "If you are born poor that is not your fault, but if you die poor that is your fault." Being poor does not have to refer to just money, but happiness, love, and impact. Think of poor as lack of something. What you desire to hold is your goal that should not be influenced by your environment, background, or current situation. Where you are now is not the end, but just one page of your book called life. Your passion understands what it takes, so follow the light at the end of the tunnel. Light does exist where dark resides. Be the person you look up to and become the CEO of your life.

Lessons are blessings in disguise. Never take them for face value, instead apply the lessons where they best fit. One of the most impactful exercises I have been a part of was writing down who I would be if I did not have any roadblocks to stop me like money, people, and things. Look for who you sincerely want to be and be that. You give off an energy field of passion and purpose when you follow the path that makes you genuinely happy. If you do what you love, you will forget that it is payday. These five lessons are to inspire you because your set purpose is just the beginning of positive change in the world.

Made in the USA
Columbia, SC
15 June 2019